PREFACE

It is with great pleasure that I commend this booklet to the publi [illegible] an important part of our local heritage; its history should be of in [illegible] live in and around the Wandle Valley and more evidence of that history still remains than many realise. The proper conservation of all aspects of the river must concern us all.

The Wandle still has an important role to play in the modern landscape; it yet has stretches of considerable natural beauty, especially where it flows through public parks, to which it lends charm and character. The policy of the Boroughs concerned, and the G.L.C., of opening up linking riverside walks will, as time goes on, greatly increase the importance of the river in leisure activities.

The idea of the Wandle Group to co-ordinate activities of organisations interested in the river and its history was initiated by a Wandsworth head-teacher, Mr. Royston Twilley, and our thanks are due to him and the Group for producing the first comprehensive guide to the river for 50 years. The London Borough of Sutton is pleased to be associated.

R. J. SLATER, A.R.I.C.S., A.S.V.A.
Chairman, Leisure and Recreation Committee
London Borough of Sutton

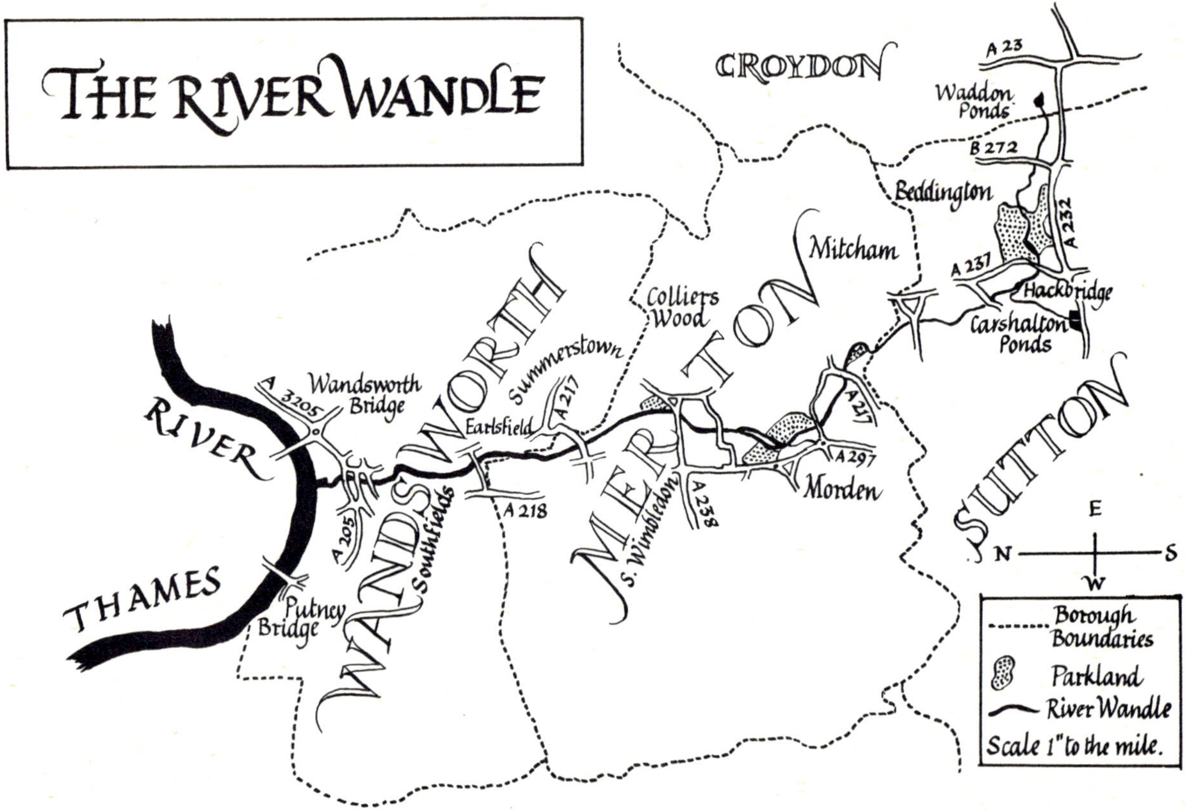
THE RIVER WANDLE
CROYDON
A 23
Waddon Ponds
B 272
Beddington
A 232
Mitcham
A 237
Hackbridge
Carshalton Ponds
Colliers Wood
MERTON
SUTTON
Summerstown
A 217
Wandsworth Bridge
A 3205
RIVER
THAMES
WANDSWORTH
Earlsfield
A 218
A 205
Southfields
S. Wimbledon
A 238
A 297
Morden
Putney Bridge
E
N
S
W
Borough Boundaries
Parkland
River Wandle
Scale 1" to the mile.

List of Contributors

Mr. D. J. S. CLUETT, A.L.A. (*Senior Reference Librarian, London Borough of Sutton*).
Mr. J. JACKSON (*Teacher, Earlsfield Junior Mixed School, S.W.18*).
Miss E. M. JOWETT, M.A. (*Merton Historical Society*).
Mr. A. R. KNIGHT (*Warden, Spencer Park Teachers' Centre, S.W.18*).
Mr. K. MERCER (*Planning Department, London Borough of Sutton*).
Mr. R. A. MICHELL (*Beddington, Carshalton and Wallington Archaeological Society*).
Mr. C. J. MONK (*Croydon Friends of the Earth*).
Mr. E. N. MONTAGUE, D.P.A. (*Surrey Archaeological Society*).
Mr. R. A. SHAW, A.L.A. (*Local History Librarian, London Borough of Wandsworth*).
Mrs. W. SIBTHORPE (*Watermeads Trust*).
Mr. P. SOWAN, B.Sc. (*Croydon Natural History and Scientific Society*).
Mr. C. A. TOASE, A.L.A. (*Senior Reference Librarian, London Borough of Merton*).
Mr. D. J. TURNER, B.Sc. (*Surrey Archaeological Society*).
Mr. R. C. TWILLEY (*Head, Earlsfield Junior Mixed School, S.W.18*).
Professor M. J. WILKS, M.A., Ph.D. (*Carshalton Society*).

Artwork and Design SHIRLEY EDWARDS
(*London Borough of Sutton Public Libraries*)

Printed by
Fleetwing Press, Wallington

THE RIVER WANDLE

A guide and handbook

Compiled by the Wandle Group

Edited by Royston Twilley and Michael Wilks

London Borough of Sutton Public Libraries

London Borough of Sutton Public Libraries
Central Library,
Manor Park Road, Sutton, Surrey, SM1 4AH

First published 1974

ISBN 0 9503224 1 5

FOREWORD

This is the first attempt to provide a short handbook and guide to the whole of the River Wandle. As such, it does not seek to compete with a full-length study like J. M. Hobson's *Book of the Wandle*. But Hobson's work is now half a century old, and the condition and appearance of the river and its surroundings have changed very considerably during the intervening period. At the same time interest in the history of the river, and the desire to protect and improve its amenities, have been growing steadily in recent years, and numerous groups and organisations are now concerned with different aspects of it. The expedient has therefore been adopted of asking the member societies of the Wandle Group to pool their information, and the present booklet is a composition of the expert knowledge which each has supplied. A reading list and guide to other material is included, but students and readers with more specialised interests are advised to contact the individual societies listed for further information.

The Editors wish to express their appreciation to Mr. Douglas Cluett as Chairman of the Wandle Group and its publications sub-committee, and to all those who have provided the substance of the following pages whose names are listed inside the front cover. Apologies will no doubt be necessary for many imperfections, but it is hoped to produce a revised edition of the handbook and guide at regular intervals.

R.C.T.
M.J.W.

Waddon Ponds, Croydon, are the point at which the Wandle appears for the first time, after passing under Croydon. This is all that remains of a much larger manorial mill pond, in which Nelson is said to have fished. *Photo by D. J. Cluett*

CONTENTS

Carew Manor and Beddington Church, viewed from the East, as drawn by Joseph Nash c. 1830. This shows the back of the late XVth century Great Hall, although the rest of the house was substantially rebuilt in 1709 and again when used as an orphanage after the sale of 1859. *Collection of Sutton Public Libraries*

THE WANDLE

The name Wandle appears to be a back formation from Wandsworth—the *Wendleswurth* or Wendel's settlement of 693—and as such did not develop until the end of the medieval period, whereas the name of the river itself from the seventh century onwards was the *hlidaburna,* meaning either the loud (*hlyde*) or sloping (*hlid*) stream. Either reading might be appropriate to a river with the relatively sharp average drop of about 15ft. per mile over the dozen miles of its length from Croydon to Wandsworth. This name was steadily corrupted, appearing as Ledeborne in 1230 and Lovebourn in 1349. Wandle (or its variants like Wandal and Wandell) seems to have been in use by the sixteenth century, although the first known use is Camden's attempt to latinise it as Vandalis in 1586. This does not justify the common assumption that Vandalis was the original Roman name of the river, and, whilst it has appeared on some maps, it is mostly poets who have made use of it since.

Geological Features

It is sometimes argued that in prehistoric times the Wandle originated in the Weald and flowed northwards across the North Downs through the Merstham Gap. According to this 'Wealden Wandle' theory, the uppermost stretches of the River Mole should be seen as a survival of the headwaters of the Wandle. Evidence for this theory may be provided by the chert pebbles to be found in the Wandle gravel deposits. But these pebbles can also be accounted for by the alternative view that the chert derives from the clay with flint deposits capping the higher points of the Downs themselves, and most writers have accepted that the Wandle originates entirely from the chalk covering the Downs. Rainwater percolating through the chalk sinks down until it reaches a depth where the rock is saturated with water: but at various places lower down the chalk slopes this level or water table meets the surface at the point where the chalk joins the overlying Tertiary beds of the Wandle Valley. This produces a line of springs along the north side of the Downs running westwards from Croydon through Waddon, Beddington and Carshalton, and the ponds in which these springs are to be found mark the effective beginning of the river.

Behind these springs lies a series of dry valleys running up into the Downs. The coombes at the tops of the valleys have been beheaded by the northwards erosion and recession of the chalk escarpment. The Merstham Gap may itself be an example of this, and other beheaded coombes can or will eventually be seen to the north of Godstone and Reigate, and in the Lower Kingswood area. The valleys have for the most part been dry during the period of recorded history, and have been used since Roman times for roads and, more recently, for railways. But they previously contained streams of some size, and still provide deposits of river gravel along their floors. Here again the origin of these valleys has been the subject of much debate. The most widely accepted explanation is that they were formed by the normal erosion of the streams themselves: although it has recently been suggested that they are the result of karst processes, but that their forms have been obscured by periglacial features, both erosional and depositional.

It is possible that the valleys south of Carshalton—one behind Carshalton Park and the other at Banstead Road—retained surface water until the end of the medieval period, and it was accepted down to the late eighteenth century that the Carshalton Wandle was the main branch of the river, the Croydon arm being regarded as no more than a tributary. But the priority of the eastern branch is now generally recognised, and a study of the sources of the Wandle properly begins with the Caterham and Smitham Bottom valleys south of Croydon. These are not always dry, since heavy rainfall in the autumn and winter produces temporary surface flows of excess water in the following spring known as bournes. Traditionally, but incorrectly, said to flow every seven years and to foretell disasters (hence the old name 'woe-waters'), these are best exemplified by the Caterham bourne, which last flowed in 1968-69. This takes the form of a line of springs extending from the Woldingham Road by the Mumbles railway viaduct down to Whyteleafe and Kenley, from where a combination of open ditches and culverts leads northwards through Purley to Croydon. But the only remnant to be found in Croydon itself is the Royal Oak pond in Brighton Road. The less well known Coulsdon bourne can also be traced from near Hooley to the Red Lion at Coulsdon. Further along in Carshalton the appearance of bourne waters has been recorded in Carshalton Park and in the Westmead and Wrythe streams north-west of Carshalton House, but not in the present century.

From Croydon onwards, where the Wandle Valley opens out, wide spreads or outwash fans of sands and gravel have been laid out by the river along the valley floor. The greater part of these deposits is roughly worn flints from the chalk higher upstream, and more rounded flints and sands from the Blackheath Pebble beds, Thanet Sand and other Tertiary strata above the chalk. Geological survey has tentatively divided the Wandle gravels into three groups, and correlated them with the Boyn Hill (oldest and highest), Taplow, and Flood Plain (youngest and lowest) terraces of the Thames. This correlation was mainly based on altitude, and more recent work has concentrated on obtaining more precise dating of the gravels from their fossil contents. Large mammal remains have been of little assistance in this respect, but a recent discovery of fossiliferous peat with wood fragments and insect remains from within the gravels in Beddington Park yielded a radio-carbon date of about 8,000 years B.C. This helped to produce an authoritative review of the two uppermost gravel terraces, the Fairfield and Mitcham terraces, for which a detailed entomological study supported a late glacial date, and offered evidence of 'a rigorous climate in which temporary pools or marshy areas became colonised by such vegetation as mosses, sedges, and small willows' (Peak and Osborne, 1971).

Natural History

Although the Wandle can no longer offer the naturalist the numerous varieties of plant and animal life listed in Smee (1872) and Hobson (1924), many species can still be found in the less polluted reaches of the upper parts of the river. Traditionally the Wandle was a rich source of watercress, and at Carshalton a twelfth-century version of the village name as Kersalton (= Cress Alton) indicates that extensive beds were already in existence at that time. Water-cress plants are still to be seen here, and there were also flourishing beds on the north bank of the river at Richmond

Green, Beddington. The banks of the Croydon branch also provide wild celery, and this arm of the river is thickly populated with starwort, Canadian pondweed and potamogeton, especially in the richest part between Carew Manor, Beddington, and The Grange at Wallington. Similarly, the plant populations around Carshalton Ponds and The Grove are very rich indeed, and include starwort and Canadian pondweed. But the industrial estates then begin to take their toll, and at the point where the waters of the Carshalton and Croydon branches meet plant life is almost completely absent on the Carshalton side.

On leaving the confluence and walking down the Wandle it is clear that plants do not show until well past the Culvers Mill site, where there is again potamogeton, starwort and Canadian pondweed, with wild celery on the banks. Although the sewage effluent from Beddington which joins the Wandle at Goat Green has a marked effect on the plants, they are to be found as far down as Watermeads, where the plants once more begin to build up to some extent. After Mitcham, however, the plants do not show very strongly, except in the back waters in Morden Park, and after this the Wandle is dead so far as plants are concerned from Morden Park down to the Thames.

The plants control the small animals that live in the ecosystem by affording them both food and shelter, and there is still sufficient plant life in the upper parts of the river to support many fish. Three-spined stickleback, miller's thumb and common loach are plentiful in Carshalton Ponds and in the stream through The Grove. But it is doubtful whether the Wandle could now support any of the larger species of fish which gave the river its reputation, so that in 1817 it was said that the privately-owned stretches of the Wandle provided as good angling as anywhere in the country. This had already been recognised by the monarchy: the Wandle Valley was declared a royal hunting and fishing preserve in 1606 (to Merton, extended to Croydon in 1634). From Camden, Izaac Walton and Thomas Fuller onwards, the trouts at Carshalton 'with marble spots like a tortoise' were famous for their excellence. Huge catches are recorded in eighteenth- and nineteenth-century accounts, and good examples of Wandle trout (a Rainbow Trout caught in about 1895, and a brown trout caught in 1905) can be seen at Wallington Library. Another particularly good section of the river for trout fishing was that above Watermeads, where the fishing rights were owned by a private angling society, the Wandle Fisheries Association. But from the middle of the nineteenth century there were increasing complaints about worsening river conditions, and the last recorded catch of Carshalton trout was at Shepley in 1913, although they are said to have been seen for some years after that.

In turn both plants and animals support the aquatic birds like swans, ducks, coots and moorhens, and there are only good numbers of these birds in areas where the flora is particularly rich. Most of the birds that will be seen along the river are the typical suburban species such as blackbirds, thrushes, starlings, woodpigeons, sparrows, tits and wrens. But the wilder parts of the river—Beddington Park and the Sewage Farm, the Hackbridge area, Watermeads and Morden Park—also support the common summer migrants like the willow warbler, the garden warbler, the blackcap and the lesser whitethroat; and areas of open ground like playing fields and parks have great numbers of feeding gulls of several kinds that congregate at these places before moving off to the reservoirs around London Airport. Special mention should be made of the Beddington Sewage Farm at Hackbridge, which, because of its undisturbed nature, is one of the best places for birdwatching in London. Although the fields are no longer regularly flooded, and cannot therefore support the tremendous population of wading birds that were once to be seen there, the ditches and settling tanks enable lapwing and redshank to breed there, whilst the fields provide winter feeding grounds for gulls, lapwings and starlings. The starlings also use Watermeads as a collecting point before they move up to their central London roosting sites, but this woodland bird sanctuary, together with the adjacent Happy Valley, provides shelter for many other types, and the heron and kingfisher can still be seen here on occasions. Ornithologists are also advised to note the many kinds of birds in the trees of the churchyard behind Carshalton Ponds.

Since the Wandle flows through a succession of parks, many fine specimens of trees can be seen along its route. Large limes, elms and horse chestnuts are a special feature, and many examples can be seen in Beddington Park. The Grange has a bent old mulberry tree and several Wellingtonia. The Grove also has a number of specimen trees, and the largest known London plane stands by the Upper Pond. Further down the river the island at The Culvers has a fine collection of trees, affording a particularly beautiful view from the road bridge, and these include an old specimen of the cork oak, a southern European species very uncommon in this country. Watermeads consists mainly of willows, alder, elder and hawthornes, but both Ravensbury Park and Morden Hall Park have many interesting trees, and the former contains some particularly handsome plane trees. But a complete tree survey for the whole length of the Wandle is urgently needed.

Archaeology

From time to time the river yields traces of fossilised early animal remains. The most notable finds have been in the Croydon gravels (1897, 1906, 1921), where mammal species included grizzly bear, red deer and roe deer, reindeer, Irish elk, mammoth, horse, hippopotamus, rhinoceros, lion, hyena and bison. A rhinoceros skull was found in Carshalton Ponds in 1899. But greater significance attaches to the traces of early human occupation, and evidence for the prehistory of man tends to be found more densely in river valleys than elsewhere, partly because the river has itself moved and redeposited this material, and partly because the rivers formed natural and recognisable lines of communication. Implements from the Old Stone Age (the Palaeolithic Period) in Britain are almost exclusively found in river gravels laid down during the Ice Age. The Wandle Valley is no exception, and tools have been found in the gravel terraces of the primeval Thames and Wandle, now cut through by the modern rivers and their tributaries: a large number of Palaeolithic implements come from the area around St. Anne's Church, Wandsworth.

With the passing of the Ice Age, there comes the Mesolithic period or Middle Stone Age (7,000 to 4,000 B.C. in Britain) when men still depended on hunting and fishing, and so favoured dry sites close to rivers and lakes for occupation. Numerous characteristic implements from this period have been found around the headwaters of the

Carshalton Ponds in 1952, looking across to All Saints' Parish Church, part of which dates back to about 1200. Queen's Well, the XVIIth century house shown here, was demolished in 1963 and replaced by the present old people's homes. The Ponds originally served the manorial corn mill at Stone Court. *Photo by Croydon Times*

Wandle at Waddon, Beddington and Carshalton, usually on the dry, lightly wooded soils of the Thanet Sand beds overlooking the spring line. The debris of a camp site at Orchard Hill, just south of Carshalton Ponds, was excavated during 1964-65, and produced over 15,000 pieces of struck flint and large numbers of fishbones. But Neolithic or New Stone Age man was able to introduce the knowledge of farming to Britain, together with technological innovations like the use of pottery and the manufacture of stone cutting tools by grinding and polishing. Settlement by these new farmers, from about 4,000 B.C. onwards, was largely confined to the thinner soils of chalk and limestone hills and the lighter gravels of the river valleys. Neolithic tools have been found around the Wandle, and Neolithic pottery at Mitcham, but the Valley as a whole seems to have been only intermittently inhabited at this time.

Knowledge of metallurgy reached Britain fitfully, and there is no clear break between the Neolithic and Bronze Ages. Bronze-using peoples of the second millenium B.C. are known to have inhabited the river valleys of Surrey, and important hoards of bronze implements—probably deposited by itinerant bronze-smiths—have been found at Beddington and Carshalton. At the mouth of the Wandle in the Wandsworth Gas Works area large numbers of Bronze Age weapons have been dredged from the silts of both rivers, and it is possible that these were votive offerings to a river god. Bronze and brass figures found in the river at Carshalton in 1794 may however be of a much later date. The introduction of iron tools and weapons seems to have made little difference at first, although evidence for military use slowly accumulates. That steps were taken to defend certain key positions along the river is shown by the number of fortified enclosures of this Iron Age period: at Beddington (Brandybottle Hill), Wallington (Bunkers Field), Carshalton (Queen Mary's Hospital and west of Banstead Road, which may suggest that streams were still running past these sites), and Wimbledon. Nothing now remains to be seen of these encampments, except for the bank and ditch of the small hillfort on Wimbledon golf course; but mention should also be made of the remarkable series of underground chambers leading down towards Waddon Ponds with evidence of Iron Age (and later) occupation discovered during house-building in 1902. Various Iron Age artifacts have also been found on St. Ann's Hill, Wandsworth, and at the mouth of the river, and a fine enamelled shield from Battersea is now in the British Museum.

Subsequently the Romans settled in the Valley, and a villa bathhouse and burials are recorded at Beddington Sewage Farm and Church respectively. There is also a late Romano-British burial and habitation site on the Willow Lane factory estate downstream from Goat Bridge; and traces of another were found south-west of Merton Bridge (Lombard Road factory estate) during gravel-digging in 1922. The Roman road Stane Street from London to Chichester crossed the Wandle near Merton Bridge, and there was a wayside market on the west bank near Deer Park Road, Morden. Roman roads also passed through Croydon, one probably crossing the Wandle between Waddon Ponds and Purley Way, and it is possible that there was another settlement in this area. Scattered finds of Roman material have been made in Wallington and Carshalton, and in Wandsworth, where recent excavation has brought to light a settlement at Putney and a north-south road leading to the Thames. The three-mile long earthwork from Purley to the Wandle at the

Croydon-Sutton borough boundary at Waddon, known as the Merebank, may be either a Roman road or an Anglo-Saxon boundary bank. Saxon mercenaries were introduced into Southern England to defend it against invaders at the end of the Roman occupation, and some of the first were settled at Croydon and Mitcham (Morden Road) to hold the approaches to London. Their cemeteries have been excavated, and the cemetery at Beddington Park may also originate from the same cause: it is possible that there was another at Carshalton House; but the cemetery discovered in the eighteenth century by Merton Bridge probably commemorates the battle of Meretun in 871 between Ethelred of Wessex and the Viking leader Guthram. Once brought in, the Saxons stayed to rule, and Anglo-Saxon villages then grew up at Croydon, Beddington, Wallington, Carshalton and Mitcham.

Historic Houses

Whilst it was the distribution of the Anglo-Saxon villages along the river which largely determined the siting of the manors recorded in Domesday, it was the picturesque setting of the river itself which brought about the transformation of these manorial lands in the later Middle Ages into a series of large mansions and pleasure grounds laid out along its banks. To an important extent the history of the Wandle is the story of its great houses, and even today it is still possible to traverse much of the length of the river above Wimbledon in a series of jumps from one ancient demesne to the next. Relatively few of these estates retain anything approaching their medieval form, but only Wallington has almost completely disappeared beneath the spread of modern housing and industrial estates. Quite a number, including Ravensbury and Waddon, have left us parks, even if little trace of the succession of manor houses which once stood in them remains; and one or two still have the old parish churches attached to them. The best example is Carew Manor, Beddington, with its Tudor Great Hall embedded in a nineteenth-century building, and flanked by the largely fifteenth-century church. Similarly the manor of Stone Court at Carshalton, now represented only by a small part of the eighteenth-century house, has the parish church, dating from the twelfth century, separated from it only by one of the Ponds.

If these examples reflect the tradition of lay patronage of ecclesiastical property, the converse is provided by the manors of Merton and Morden, which were both owned by abbeys during the medieval period. Merton Priory (1114-1538) occupied some sixty acres south of Merton High Street, and the southern boundary wall and gateway can still be seen in Station Road, but the banks of the river through the grounds were soon taken over for milling and calico-printing. The manor of Morden on the other hand, owned by Westminster Abbey until the Dissolution of the monasteries, remained in the keeping of the Garth family from the sixteenth to the nineteenth century, thus preserving Morden Hall (partly c. 1700) and the Deer Park surrounding the house and a good stretch of the river. Further south at Hackbridge both Merton and St. Mary Overy (Southwark) had extensive lands which came in course of time to form the Culvers and Shepley House estates—subsequently used extensively for industry, and now built over—but which lasted into the present century as examples of the way in which the river was deliberately used as ornamentation for a country house. As one writer put it in 1889, the upper Wandle had become the pet of the wealthy: 'No longer does it flood its watercress beds and turn vulgar mill wheels, but now winds through lovely gardens where money and ingenuity are devoted to developing its beauties, where bowers and charming vistas, rustic bridges, glens, glades and varied vegetation form a fit setting for its crystal loveliness.' One may recall in this context how water from the Wandle was led into the grounds of Merton Place, purchased for Nelson by Lady Hamilton, and laid out as a miniature representation of the Nile.

At first these estates, carved out of the old manorial extents, had been created by members of the aristocracy and leading government servants who found it convenient to have a rural retreat close to London. But by the seventeenth and eighteenth centuries they were largely the preserve of prosperous City businessmen, merchants and lawyers, or senior army and navy officers, who relished the prospect of a double life as country squires, and most places can offer some of the smaller houses with which they lined the river banks. Half a dozen are perhaps worth special mention. At Wallington there is the early eighteenth-century Wandle Bank (later owned by the artist Arthur Hughes), and the visitor should cross the river to The Grange, which has lost its first house but keeps something of Smee's famous garden. At Carshalton one of the best houses, Strawberry Lodge (c. 1700), has now lost its riverside garden, but the early nineteenth-century Grove house is still surrounded by its park, and the springs of the Wandle should be traced on one side to the grounds of the outstanding Carshalton House (also c. 1700) and on the other to the site of Carshalton Park House in Carshalton Park. One of the finest houses on the river, Mitcham Grove, associated with Lord Clive and the banker Henry Hoare, now leaves only a field, but further downstream the Regency Morden Lodge and the early eighteenth-century Wandle Villa (with adjacent folly) at Phipps Bridge are well worth stopping to admire. Wandle Park, just north of Merton High Street, preserves the location of Wandle Bank House, whose owner, James Perry, friend of Nelson, also possessed the nearby mill. Most of the proprietors of these estates had no objection to taking a share in the profits which the riverside industries could also offer them, and the history of their houses cannot be separated from that of the mills alongside them. As Hassell so aptly put it in 1817, the Wandle was seen to possess many charms: 'it can boast of giving a splendour to trade and a repose from its fatigues; every quarter of a mile its course is accompanied by elegant chateaus, and obstructed by commerce—mills succeed each other at short distances down the whole stream.'

Industrial Archaeology

The fast flowing waters of the Wandle, with a markedly higher average fall per mile in its upper reaches, made the river useless for navigation but ideal for mills. The water-powered corn mill dates back to the later Roman empire, and Domesday Book records at least thirteen of these mills on the Wandle—more than half of them above Mitcham—and it is almost certain that downland parishes like Woodmansterne and Banstead also had their mills down in the river valley. The row of ponds along the river from Croydon to Carshalton were used as millponds from a very early date,

The Fishermen's Cottages, Mitcham, seen from the Watermeads. The cottages were built about 1760, and recall the importance of the Wandle as a trout stream. The Watermeads were acquired by the National Trust as a riverside walk and bird sanctuary in 1913.
Photo by J. Jackson

but most of the innumerable canals, cuts and sluices on the rest of the river seem to be of post-medieval origin. By 1600 there were no less than 24 corn mills on the Wandle, and at both ends of it one can find mills which ground corn continuously from the Norman Conquest to the late nineteenth or early twentieth century: at Croydon, Waddon and Carshalton; and the immense flour mills of Wandsworth, the lowest of which was a tide-mill.

The number of mills was increased by the development of the fulling mill for clothmaking c. 1200; and of the dye-wood grinding mills (logwood, brazilwood) resulting from the explorations of the sixteenth century. At least one Hackbridge site (Shepley) seems to have made a progression through from corn to fulling to dyewood, and eventually became a spread of four gunpowder mills in the mid-seventeenth century, which were used for other purposes after that. Similarly the Amery mills at Merton Priory began as manorial corn mills, and were successively changed through dyewood and copper to the present paperboard mill; whilst Wallington also ran the gamut from corn to fulling to cloth to paper, and ended as a chocolate factory. The major expansion of the Wandle milling industries in the early modern period owed much to the expertise of refugees from the Continent, especially those from the Low Countries and the Huguenots from France. They were mainly responsible for the development of the copper industry at Carshalton, Merton and Wimbledon. Grinding tobacco for snuff, on the other hand, may derive from Sir Walter Raleigh's residence at Mitcham, although the snuff mills mostly seem to have developed in the second half of the eighteenth century (Beddington, Carshalton, Hackbridge, Mitcham and Morden). By this time the Wandle mills had proliferated into a still greater variety of types, including leather and oil, and paper manufactories—notably the famous Ansell milling complex at the end of the century which made Carshalton into one of the most important centres of paper production in the country. Since the millowners were particularly concerned about the need to transport their produce to London for sale they supported both the scheme for a Grand Surrey Canal, proposed by Dodd in 1795 but never built, and the Surrey Iron Railway from Wandsworth to Croydon and Merstham (with a spur from Mitcham to the Hackbridge mills), the first public railway actually built in England, which operated from 1803 to 1846.

In 1805 the Wandle was said to be 'the hardest worked river for its size in the world' (Malcolm), and according to Lewis ninety mills, some with two or three wheels each, stood along it in 1831. By the nineteenth century still more types of mill are recorded: hemp and iron mills, drug grinding, silk printing, woollen and felt-making, and peppermint and lavender distilleries. But the lists of mills drawn up in the middle of the century give a false impression of continuing prosperity. The Wandle milling industries, crippled by falling water levels and the spread of the steam engine, were on the verge of collapse, and their decline in the second half of the century was rapid. So too this period saw the virtual demise of the Wandle calico industry, which had used the exceptionally pure water of the river to bleach the cloth spread out along its banks to dry in the sun. This again seems to have been introduced by Huguenot refugees in the seventeenth century, but had developed extensively all along the river after 1750, when almost the entire working population of Merton and three-quarters of that of Wandsworth were engaged in the trade. For printing the cloth, and making the copper printing plates, the main centre was the area of Merton Priory, which towards the end of the nineteenth century came to include two famous printing works, William Morris' and Arthur Liberty's, of which the latter is still operating successfully. But for bleaching the largest factory in the world was at Carshalton (The Culvers), and this was forced out of business by financial crisis and technological change in the 1850s. By then there were only 34 mills altogether still at work on the Wandle, and eventually in 1889 one writer was able to remark on the melancholy sight of a river littered with the corpses of dead industries —'the living, generally horribly unpicturesque, interspersed here and there with their dead and dying brothers'.

Modern factories, notably those manufacturing chemicals, paints, plastics, and electrical components, have now mostly taken over this valuable industrial land, and, together with suburban housing estates, have covered up many of the mill sites. But there is still a great deal which can be seen by those who are prepared to go and look for it, although it is unfortunate that very few actual waterwheels have been preserved. There are now none left in the Boroughs of Croydon and Wandsworth, and only one (The Grove, Carshalton) out of some thirty recorded sites in Sutton. Only the Borough of Merton is better provided for, with three sets of wheels in something approaching working order: at the Ravensbury and Morden Hall snuff mills, and the wheel at Liberty's printing works in Merton itself. Their last employment was in an attempt to use them to generate electricity, but their performance seems to have made it clear that they were designed for other and older purposes.

Water Control, Pollution and Conservation

Safeguarding their water supply was always a constant concern for millers and millowners, and the story of the Wandle can be seen from one point of view as a perpetual interaction of the twin problems of too little and too much water. Attempts to keep the river free from obstructions, and to build up and maintain the banks in good repair, are a constant theme in local manorial court records from the fourteenth century onwards, and a long series of instructions to landowners to keep the stream clear and prevent flooding can be found in the accounts of the Surrey and Kent Commission of Sewers during the sixteenth century. For most of the past five hundred years the danger has always been that the Wandle would become too full to contain all its water, and even in the late nineteenth century (when farmers would still deliberately flood their fields in winter to provide improvised skating rinks) old photographs reveal a volume of water in the river and its adjacent streams which seems incredible to modern eyes. Isolated instances of flooding do in fact still occur at various points along the river, and a comprehensive programme of flood-control works is at present being pursued by the Greater London and other London Borough Councils.

At the same time the presence of so many mills along the river required that it should be kept at as high a level of flow as possible, especially in times of drought: water rights were carefully set out and jealously guarded through numerous court actions. Periodic proposals to abstract water from the Wandle to serve London and its expanding suburbs met with fierce resistance—one of the earliest and best known schemes, in 1610, being to pipe one-tenth of the flow away from the river at Waddon direct to the City. Organised opposition subsequently led to the abandonment of a number of similar suggestions for creating reservoirs and sinking wells in 1833, 1843 and 1850; but a famous test case in 1859 resulted in a House of Lords decision by which Croydon obtained a judgement against local millowners that landowners also had the ownership of underground water in the land and the right to drain it off. At this period (1861) the flow of the river at Wandsworth was measured as being 84 million gallons a day, but from then onwards it was clear that this would tend to diminish steadily as more and more water had to be extracted to supply the rapidly rising populations of South London. The sort of effect that this could produce was shown in 1906 when a London, Brighton and South Coast Railway well sunk at Carshalton reduced the springs to half flow and brought about a drop of a foot in the general level of the river after only two days of test pumping. This confirmed that the water table had been falling as the suburbs advanced southwards, and the problem of a failing water supply, which had already reached Mitcham by the end of the previous century, was seriously affecting Carshalton by the 1920s. The Ponds here were completely dry during the drought of 1921-22; the springs failed again in 1934-35 and 1944-45; and this became a regular occurrence during the 1950s and early 1960s. The years 1966-69, however, afforded an interesting comparison between two contrasting methods of dealing with this situation. At Wandle Park, Croydon (purchased as a public amenity in 1890) the lake was filled in and the river crossing the park was put into an underground pipe. This converted Wandle Park into a park without a Wandle, and for effective purposes the eastern branch of the river now begins at Waddon. At Carshalton on the other hand the western branch was safeguarded by a waterproofing scheme for the Ponds, which are now kept artificially full by a recirculating system reaching down to Goat Bridge, and it is hoped to extend this scheme to Margaret's Pool during 1975.

In the past local authorities have tended to act primarily as drainage authorities in their dealings with the Wandle, considering it essentially from a public health standpoint. That this has been a historical necessity is not open to doubt. The population growth during the nineteenth century far outstripped the capacity of parish and town councils to provide adequate waste disposal and refuse collection facilities, so that by the middle of the century the ponds and channels of the river were little better than open sewers, and a major contributory factor to the spread of disease. Thus, after particularly bad outbreaks of cholera and typhoid in the late 1840s, much of the Wandle through Croydon was culverted and the ponds filled in. An improved water supply was obtained from new boreholes sunk into the chalk, and in 1860 the Beddington Sewage Farm was established—which solved Croydon's sewage problem but, by discharging effluent into the river at Beddington Corner, helped to make the Wandle into the most polluted river in London. Meanwhile, an attempt to cover over the Wandle along Carshalton High Street was defeated by local opposition (and this was not to be achieved until the late 1920s), and John Ruskin led a campaign during the 1860s and 1870s to restore the purity of the Wandle springs. But throughout the last century extensive culverting

One of the channels into which the Wandle was cut as it crossed the Deer Park at Morden Hall to serve the mills and manufactories at Phipps Bridge. Morden Hall was the home of the Garth family, and the Park now owned by the National Trust, is open to the public. *Photo by D. J. Cluett*

has continued to take place down the whole length of the river, especially along the Merton, Wimbledon and Wandsworth sections, and at many points the river has either been lowered into a safer, more easily cleaned, but aesthetically unattractive concrete channel, or diverted altogether—a good example being the major alteration of the river's course between Goat Bridge and Watermeads carried out during the 1950s and early 1960s. New plant installed in the Beddington Sewage Farm soon afterwards has, however, now greatly improved the quality of the effluent, a vital consideration when it is borne in mind that on occasions the percentage of effluent in the river below this area can rise as high as 90%, and that the river has still to receive the outflow from the Wandle Valley Sewage Works at Byegrove Road. Moreover far too much industrial waste, especially oil, cyanide and other chemicals, still finds its way into the river, and there is little point in trying to restock the river with fish whilst this continues.

If therefore the first priority must be to maintain the flow of water in the Wandle, much more needs to be done to ensure that its potential as an environmental benefit is fully realised and used. In 1890 a party of anglers visiting Carshalton were so disgusted with the condition of Pope's 'blue, transparent Vandalis' that, following the example of American societies, they formed a company with a capital of £5,000 to clear the river of rubbish and pollution down to Wandsworth (although they accepted that this final section was already beyond redemption). The River Wandle Open Spaces Committee did notable work before 1914 and again during the 1920s to create stretches of riverside walk, which it was hoped would eventually cover the entire length of the river; and the National Trust has made immensely valuable contributions by its acquisition of Watermeads (1913), Happy Valley (1915), and the Morden Hall estate (1941-43); but otherwise there were only scattered and sporadic attempts to promote riverside improvements until the end of the 1960s. In 1969, however, the Greater London Council, acting on a suggestion from the London Borough of Sutton, established the River Wandle Liaison Group, which also includes representatives from the London Boroughs of Merton and Wandsworth, aided by specialist advisers, and ready to purchase land for footpath extensions and discuss joint action to deal with any problems concerning the river. Plans to transform the Wandle into an amenity and leisure area are gradually being put together, assisted by the proposals put forward by local conservation societies. The Wandle Group was formed in 1973 to co-ordinate the activities of these societies and to bring about full co-operation between the local authorities and the public at large in their efforts to secure the future well-being of the River Wandle.

Croydon

Most people wishing to walk along the Wandle will probably begin at Waddon Ponds, which is all that can be seen of the Wandle in Croydon today despite the fact that they are close to the point where the river leaves the Borough. It is not however difficult to trace the line which the river once took when it flowed through the centre of Croydon itself.

The Wandle rose in South Croydon near the Swan and Sugarloaf, and there were two or three ponds between the main Brighton Road and Haling Cottage in the grounds of what is now Whitgift School. The stream then ran northwards along the west side of Brighton Road, behind the Blue Anchor public house, and along Southbridge Road. It divided into two branches in the meadow to the east of Southbridge Road, but these rejoined in front of the north door of St. Andrew's Church. The stream was now about twenty feet wide, and had two bridges across it, but was considerably increased by the strong spring opposite the west end of Sheldon Street. After what is now the Old Town roundabout it again divided to enclose a marshy area known as Bog Island, and then flowed into the grounds of Croydon Palace. Croydon had been a manor of the archbishops of Canterbury from before the Norman Conquest, and the Palace was built to give the medieval archbishops a residence conveniently close to London. It was sold in 1758, but parts of it, notably the Great Hall (c. 1450), remain in use as a girls' school and can be visited at certain times. During the late eighteenth and first half of the nineteenth centuries there was a calico factory here, and the grounds south of the Palace along the river were used for bleaching.

The area around the Palace and Scarbrook Hill contained powerful springs which turned it into a maze of ponds, streams and canals. There were two important ponds in Scarbrook Road. One, by the junction with Wandle Road, drained along a stream on the west side of Church Road into the Palace gardens, where it formed a series of artificial fishponds and canals before linking up with the main course of the river to the south in front of the old archway leading into the former graveyard of the Parish Church. The other, on the site of the present Technical College annexe, drained northwards into Lauds Pond by way of another stream. Lauds Pond, whose name may refer to the archbishop but is probably a corruption of 'My Lord's pond', stood behind the present supermarket (Tesco's) in Church Street. From there the water crossed Church Street by the north wall of the Elis Davy Almshouses to join up with the main stream of the Wandle. This had the effect of making the area containing the Palace, the Parish Church and the Almshouses into an island.

Apart from the Palace, already mentioned, the visitor would be well advised to look at the almshouses, founded by Elis Davy (d. 1455), and the Parish Church. There was a church here before the Conquest, but it was the medieval church built between 1380 and 1440 which was largely destroyed by fire in 1867 and then rebuilt as the present imposing structure. It still contains some interesting remnants of the earlier building, including some notable archiepiscopal tombs. To the north of the church is the area known since 1511 as Pitlake (meaning 'stream in a hollow'), which served as the Croydon terminus of the Surrey Iron Railway from Wandsworth. After its opening in 1803 two other branch lines spread through Croydon. One ran up the present Tamworth Road to connect with the basin of the short-lived Croydon Canal at which is now West Croydon railway station. Another formed the extension to Merstham, and ran south on an embankment—now forming Church Road—past the network of ponds and streams around the Palace.

Where the various streams connected with the main, southern, branch of the river to the west of the Parish Church there was a large sheet of water forming a millpond, and serving a corn mill with Domesday origins. The final form of the mill was built shortly after 1800 and only lasted until 1849, when the Croydon Board of Health, in its efforts to stamp out cholera and typhoid, undertook a major campaign to fill in the ponds and culvert the streams. The brick culverts had open joints so that they could drain off surface water, and the Wandle culvert, running along the line of Old Town Road, was largely reconstructed in the 1960s. Excavation of Lauds Pond indicates that the ponds were filled up with any rubbish that came to hand.

After the millpond the combined branches of the river ran north-west across the Croydon-Epsom railway line (opened for steam engines in 1847, but previously intended to be an atmospheric railway) into two marshy fields known as Frogg Mead and Stubbs Mead. These were bought by Croydon Council from the Church Commissioners and opened as Wandle Park in 1890. The level of the park was raised by tipping to drain it; springs were used to form a boating lake; and the river was given a walk beside willow trees on its banks. However the gradual fall in the water table dried up the flow of water so frequently that in 1966-68 the lake was filled in for football pitches, and the river put into an underground pipe across the park. The only traces of what once existed are the double line of trees and the exceptional wetness of the football pitches.

The river then left the park by the bridge under the Croydon-Mitcham railway line, but now continues underground all the way through the Waddon Gas Works, where again there were calico bleaching grounds in the early nineteenth century, to flow westwards under the modern Purley Way. This probably represents the line of a local Roman road branching off the main London-Brighton Way, although the old road which Purley Way replaced twisted round the double right-angles of Waddon Court Road. This now provides the most convenient entrance to the small park containing Waddon Ponds. These represent all that remains of a much larger millpond, which was bisected by Mill Lane. The river originally flowed into the no longer extant northern pond, but was diverted at the end of the last century to the east and north of the pond. The area of land thereby created was used first for watercress beds, then for allotments, and finally for industrial use. Eventually the river was culverted through the factory estate in 1964, and the northern millpond was filled in.

The present, southern, millpond (in which Nelson is reputed to have fished) stood in the grounds of Waddon Court. The mill was a manorial corn mill, standing to the north-west of Mill Lane on the other pond. It closed down in 1928 when most of the Waddon Court estate was sold off for housing, leaving only the present 8½-acre park.

Sutton

After visiting Waddon Ponds one should leave by the public footpath leading off Mill Lane at the north-west corner of the park. This takes one between the houses and the factories to the culvert on the Croydon-Sutton boundary where the Wandle proper emerges into view for the first time. The culvert is a large one, capable of taking several times the amount of water likely to drain off Waddon Ponds, and this is to enable it to cope with the surface water absorbed by the culvert under Croydon, which can produce temporary rushes of large quantities of extremely dirty water after storms. Thus the river begins with a permanent source of pollution.

The Borough boundary, between The Ridgeway and Aldwick Road, has been roughly drawn along the line of the Merebank, which runs for three miles southwards from the Wandle to a junction of ancient tracks at Russell Hill in Purley. The bank was about four feet high, and thirty across, and was probably a Roman road used as a boundary during the Anglo-Saxon period. On the opposite (northern) bank, now Richmond Green, there were watercress beds until the 1930s: but keep to the path along the south bank which leads along to Bridlepath, and takes one round to the site of Beddington mill. This was a manorial mill dating back to Domesday, grinding corn for most of its working life, but converted to Lambert's snuff mill for most of the eighteenth and nineteenth centuries. The wheels were on the north side of the present tall building, and the river can be seen issuing from beneath the mill and Wandle Road. Here, at the end of Bridges Lane, there is the picturesque setting of the old buildings known as the Brandries on one side, and the row of cottages (Mount Pleasant) across the river but connected to their front gardens by small bridges. Continue along Wandle Bank and past the Fords to cross the main road, Hilliers/Beddington Lane.

At this point the river does a double bend north and west, and one should cross to the housing estate on the north bank, which can be entered through a gap leading into Mallinson Road. Follow this round to Crispin Crescent, where some twenty yards along on the left an alleyway between the houses will again lead alongside the river to the rear of Carew Manor and Beddington Park, the home of the Carew family for five hundred years until sold in 1859, since when it has been an orphanage and a school. Celebrated for its oranges, its water-closet, and its associations with Sir Walter Raleigh, the house has a Tudor Great Hall within the nineteenth-century exterior, and a fine dovecote (c. 1700) on the north side. On the south is Beddington Church, a pre-Domesday church with the present fabric mostly dating 1380-1520, except for the tower rebuilt in the first half of the nineteenth century. The Carew Chapel and brasses are well worth seeing.

The river may now be followed on either bank to The Grange, Wallington, where the manorial mill pond is now a boating lake. The mill stood at the car park by the bridge, but there was a calico factory opposite. Here there is still Alfred Smee's famous garden, although his house (1870) was burnt down in 1960 and has been replaced by a modern restaurant close to the springs. Note also Bridge House (c. 1770) across the main road, but as the river is inaccessible as it turns north to Hackbridge, it is advisable to walk south-west along London Road past a series of springs and pools which drain into the river. This takes one past Wandle Bank, an early eighteenth-century house lived in at one time by the Pre-Raphaelite painter Arthur Hughes, and Manor Cottage (c. 1800), the only remnant of Wallington Manor.

Keeping to the same direction past the Rose and Crown public house will lead by way of Westcroft Road to Carshalton High Street: there is a great deal of local historical interest which may be seen here, but only those items which have a specific connection with the Wandle will be mentioned for present purposes. The first is the Westcroft Canal (c. 1700) constructed to serve a snuff and iron mill, of which only the sluice remains, leading off on the right from the junction of Westcroft Road with the High Street. This can be followed almost down to the river; but it is preferable to trace its present underground route in the opposite direction along the High Street to Carshalton Place, where the canal can again be seen leading southwards into Carshalton Park. This former deer park was the centre of the manor when held by the Scawen and Taylor families during the eighteen and nineteenth centuries: the last manor house stood between Carshalton Place and Brookside until demolished in 1928. Of particular note now is the Grotto (1725) at the head of the canal, fed by underground springs from the stream whose path southwards into the Downs can be detected by the dip in the horizon of houses. This also connected, across the Park, with the Hogpit Pond, from which two streams led to the High Street. The course of one of these can be followed by leaving the Park at the main Ruskin Road entrance, from which a pink paved path leads down to The Square, where the Orangery (1727) of Leoni's projected Carshalton Park House still stands.

Where The Square joins the High Street one is at the corner of Carshalton Ponds, also used as a millpond, whose powerful springs are one of the main sources of the Wandle, although they are now kept permanently full by a waterproofing and recirculatory scheme introduced between 1967-69. At this point, the south-east corner, there was a hemp and grist mill which abutted the fifteenth-century house now used as a butcher's shop. This stands next to the Church, recorded in Domesday, now extensively rebuilt in a variety of styles from the eighteenth century onwards, but with a Lady Chapel dating back to 1200, some interesting brasses, and an impressive interior. Further along, past the holy well traditionally but erroneously named after Queen Ann Boleyn, there is an attractive seventeenth-century inn, The Greyhound, standing across the road from Honeywood, a house with a stream beneath it, rebuilt towards the end of the last century but incorporating parts of a thirteenth-century mill.

The water wheel at Liberty's Print Mill at Merton is one of the only two wheels on the Wandle still in working order. Calico printing works are known to have occupied the site since 1724, and it was acquired by Arthur Liberty in 1885.

Photo by J. Jackson

Continuing westwards up Pound Street takes one past Margaret's Pool, a spring landscaped by John Ruskin during the 1870s, as a stone on the site records, to the grounds of Carshalton House (c. 1700), now St. Philomena's Convent school, in which another larger pond also served a mill and fed the Wandle. The house is the best building in Carshalton and was the residence of many famous names, including Dr. John Radcliffe, Sir John Fellowes, Lord Hardwicke, Admiral Lord Anson and Thomas Walpole. There is a striking water tower (1720) in West Street where the pond drains into a watercress stream running along Festival Walk to the Ponds.

From Honeywood Walk along the north side of the upper Pond cross over North Street and through a small gate into the park formed out of the grounds of Stone Court and The Grove, connected by an eighteenth-century bridge over the river as it leaves the lower Pond. This area also formed part of the manor with Carshalton Park, although only a small part of the eighteenth-century mansion now remains as offices by the junction of North Street with Mill Lane, and the main building in the park is The Grove house (1825). Follow the river down to the millwheel (noting the millstones and Surrey Iron Railway blocks on the west bank), which marks the site of a manorial mill grinding corn until the 1880s, although the wheel was last used to generate electricity. Then comes an area of former water-cress beds, with a small brick bridge giving access to Mill Lane. The factory site renders the river inaccessible, but a walk along Mill Lane takes one past the Ansell paper and snuff mills to Butter Hill bridge (1787 but heavily rebuilt), with copper mill and calico factory sites on the other side.

Keeping to the west bank under the railway bridge and past Strawberry Lodge (c. 1700), one comes to a small concrete bridge opposite the house which leads to what is geographically one of the most important points on the Wandle, the junction of the Croydon and Carshalton branches of the river in an area of wild ground which was once part of the gardens of Shepley House. This public open space is not always accessible to the public, but it is expected that the Borough Council's proposals for a riverside walk will include this area. Shepley House (demolished 1933) stood on the west bank, and had a history going back to medieval times, and the whole of this area is thickly littered with mill sites—fulling, gunpowder, copper, leather, oil, wool and snuff—but little can now be seen except factories on the eastern bank as one progresses on the opposite side along Riverside Gardens and then a riverside path which emerges in Nightingale Road by the Hack Bridge.

Cross the bridge (a modern replacement of at least two earlier ones) to Hackbridge Road—which leads to an attractive village green with some old cottages and inn (the Red Lion)—but turn immediately north along the path on the east side of the river. At this point there was a terminus for the Surrey Iron Railway, serving the Shepley and Culvers mills. To reach the latter it is necessary to cross by the bridge to the island formed by the division of the river here, and, keeping to the left, reach Culvers Avenue by way of Culvers Retreat. This cornmill (known as Carshalton Mill) stood over the river where Culvers Avenue now crosses the western stream, close to the site of

The Culvers house, the centre of a great estate which specialised in calico production when owned by the great Quaker families of the Reynolds and the Gurneys.

A few yards to the left on the westernmost bank will be found the beginning of a footpath which will lead via Buckhurst Avenue right along the western bank of the river through housing and factory estates to Goat Bridge at the end of Middleton Road. Shortly before reaching the bridge a backwater creates an island on which stand the remains of Roberts leather mill and house, probably of Huguenot origin, but there is a thick cluster of mill sites round the bridge, including paper, corn, logwood, drug and peppermint mills. Across the bridge (rebuilt 1972) lies Mill Green, crossed by the outflow from the Beddington Sewage Farm on its way to join the Wandle: the Green was originally Cranemarsh in the seventeenth century, possibly a corruption of the Mitcham family name Cranmer, but ownership of the Green was in dispute between the manors of Mitcham and Wallington until well into the nineteenth century.

Merton

Below Goat Bridge the riverside path on the west bank continues towards Mitcham past a terrace of nineteenth-century cottages erected to house mill workers. In this section the course of the river is very largely man-made, having been diverted from its original bed and embanked by the Surrey County Council during the 1960s. In the course of this work two historic buildings were lost: the eighteenth-century house belonging to York's mill, which was grinding logwood for dyes as early as 1685, and was later converted into Sprules' Mitcham herb mill; and the weather-boarded building, which still had two of its three wheels, of the Foster or Searle flour mill, dating back to at least 1750 and probably replacing a medieval mill. Both were absorbed during the later nineteenth century into J. S. Deed & Sons' Eagle leather works, which still occupies a large part of the east bank at the end of Willow Lane. Note also here the small modern building which purifies the river water which is to be pumped back upstream to Carshalton Ponds by means of pipes laid along the river bed.

North of Deed's works lies an area known as Marey's Land in the fourteenth century, which became a centre of the bleaching industry in the late sixteenth and early seventeenth centuries, and remained associated with textile printing until the middle of the last century. A Romano-British habitation and burial site of the third or fourth century has also been found here. The once extensive watercress beds of this area are now rapidly being swallowed up by the Willow Lane factory estate. Meanwhile on the opposite bank the path, having reached the bend in the river known since medieval times as Bennett's Hole is obliged to diverge from the river and run up to Bishopsford Road along the edge of Poulter Park.

The reason for this is that some twelve acres of land on the west bank above Mitcham Bridge, known as the Watermeads, was given to the National Trust in 1913 to form an area of secluded walks, a bird sanctuary partly used for the growing of willows, which can only be entered by obtaining a key (50p deposit) from the Treasurer, Mr. E. J. Richardson, 97 Brookfields Avenue, Mitcham. The history of this and the surrounding area as a mill site reaches back to before the Norman Conquest. A long canal called Paper Mill Cut runs through Watermeads, but the mill has long disappeared; and all that remains of Richard Glover's early nineteenth-century snuff mill is a millstone near the bridge. Of a series of other mills (Crown Mill, Morden Mill, Grove Mill)—for flour, copper, felt and fibre—only a modern fibre factory is left on the east bank, partially masked from the river by a picturesque group of three weatherboarded 'Fishermen's Cottages' dating from 1760. This part of the Wandle was an excellent trout stream until the beginning of the present century: fishing rights were owned by the Wandle Fisheries Association, a private angling society whose bailiff lived in the wooden cottage facing the bridge.

Mitcham Bridge has a cast-iron parish boundary plate dated 1882 on the parapet facing downstream, but a bridge is shown here on a map of 1685. Until about fifty years ago a ford survived here, perhaps the 'White Ford' from which the Domesday vill of Whitford (now absorbed into Lower Mitcham) took its name. Beside the bridge an iron gate, called the Gaston Gate after a local councillor, gives access for National Trust keyholders to the path along the south-west bank through Happy Valley, two acres of riverside bird sanctuary donated to the Trust in 1915 as a memorial to Octavia Hill, one of the founders of the Trust in 1895. A door at the far end opens into Ravensbury Park, which can otherwise be entered from the Morden end of Wandle Road.

On the north-east side of the river an island of open space, used during the present century as a cricket field for Hovis Ltd., is the site of Mitcham Grove, the great house owned by the banker Henry Hoare between 1786 and 1828. The house, which replaced an Elizabethan one, was previously owned by Lord Clive of India, and was the finest in Mitcham: it was demolished in the later 1860s. The land is now scheduled for development as a Council housing estate.

On the same side of the river, but downstream from Mitcham Grove, stood the medieval manor house of Ravensbury Park, and ruins of the house demolished by Colonel Bidder in 1882 can be seen amongst the tall trees here. A new manor house was built in 1912 on the opposite (south-west) bank, but this too was demolished in the 1930s, and only the stables in Wandle Road remain. The whole area was acquired as a public park in 1930. It is believed that the main road from Mitcham to Morden crossed the river at this point until 1753.

From Ravensbury Park it is necessary to walk round by way of either Wandle Road or Morden Road to the junction of these two roads at Ravensbury snuff mill (now Whiteley Products Ltd., making sports goods). Snuff manufacture took place here from at least the middle of the eighteenth century, and the mill became famous for the 'Mitcham Shag' tobacco produced by the Rutter family, who occupied the mill from 1810 to 1925. A fine pair of wheels is still preserved in the building, and these were last used to generate electricity during the Second World War. No trace

The contrast between modern industrial usage of the Wandle and its potential for amenity and recreational purposes, is well brought out by the view from the bridge at Lydden Road, Earlsfield, which leads across to King George's Park.

Photo by J. Jackson

remains of the other Ravensbury Mill, a calico print works of the late eighteenth and nineteenth centuries, except a red brick wall by the path leading out of Ravensbury Park into Morden Road.

The river now crosses Morden Road into Morden Hall Park, which can be entered at this point. To visit the house and snuff mill, however, it is necessary to walk up Morden Hall Road, which takes one past the attractive Morden Lodge (c. 1800), also owned at one time by the Hoare family. Morden Hall itself recalls the Garth family, who built a manor house here in the mid-sixteenth century. The present building dates from c. 1700, but was extensively altered in the last century. It was sold in 1872 to Gilliat Hatfeild, whose family had already been established in the eighteenth-century snuff mill adjoining the house. The mill closed down in 1922, but one of its two wheels still remains. These buildings, which were sold to the National Trust in 1941-43, are now the London Borough of Merton Council Offices.

From the Morden Road entrance to the former deer park, it is possible to follow much of the river as it winds its way across the park through a series of divided channels. Once the river has turned north-east in a double channel, however, further progress is blocked by the Wimbledon to Croydon Railway, which cut the old road across the park when it was constructed in 1855. Leaving the north-west bank of the river, walk along the line to a footbridge over the railway, from which a footpath leads past factories to Phipps Bridge. From here it is possible to walk back along the northern watercourse, cut in 1769 by John Rucker to serve his calico-printing works, to one of the 1847 Mitcham boundary stones by the railway bridge. But it is preferable to detour southwards along Phipps Bridge Road past the row of old cottages, Everetts Place (1824), to see Wandle Villa, originally Rucker's house, which stood in front of his works. This, like the allotments alongside, which lead down to the river bank, forms part of the National Trust purchase of Morden Hall Park. Note the Coachman's Lodge in the garden on the other side of the house, and the folly beyond the cottages.

The second Mitcham mill recorded in Domesday Book may have been at Phipps Bridge, near which a mill is recorded in 1263. Today one can only see the nineteenth-century house downstream from the bridge fronting a factory which succeeds the long-established varnish and japanning works. The river must be followed on the opposite side along Phipps Bridge Road, and this can be done as far as the Windsor Avenue bridge, leading to the Lombard Road factory estate, where Roman coins and pottery were found in 1922. This is on the line of Stane Street, the Roman road from London to Chichester, which ran north to cross the Wandle at what was to become the site of Merton Priory.

The Priory (or Abbey), a house of Augustinian Canons founded in 1114, held all the land south of Merton High Street, but was almost totally demolished after the Dissolution in 1538. Part of a wall and a small gateway can be seen by continuing to the end of Phipps Bridge Road and left into Christchurch Road, and left again after the railway bridge into Station Road to the point where this road crosses the Wandle. On the south side of the bridge stands Liberty's Print Works, with a waterwheel still capable of turning, which has operated since 1885 on the site of a long line of calico and textile print factories dating back to 1724. There is still an eighteenth-century colour house here.

On the north side of the bridge the Wandle can be seen flowing past the area of William Morris' famous Merton Abbey printing works (1881-1940), again a calico site traced back to 1752. This has now been absorbed into the gigantic New Merton Board Mills, which itself replaces the medieval Amery Mills, a Domesday corn mill later converted to brazilwood grinding in the seventeenth century and copper beating in the eighteenth. But this can best be viewed from Merton High Street (reached from Station Road by way of either Abbey Road or Priory Road) where the Wandle runs along the High Street to Merton Bridge (first recorded in 1569) and joins the Pickle stream flowing in from the east along the Mitcham parish boundary. Those who go via Abbey Road will pass the eastern edge of what was once Merton Place, a house (demolished c. 1840) and estate purchased by Lady Hamilton for Nelson in 1801, which drew water from the Wandle to form streams and ponds in the garden.

Downstream from Merton Bridge the river now runs in a canal cut to serve the great eighteenth-century Merton Flour Mill, used in the present century as a leather works (Connolly Bros. Ltd.), but described in 1779 as the most complete mill in England. The old course of the river, marking the parish boundary between Mitcham and Wimbledon, can still be seen as a muddy stream meandering through Wandle Park on the east side of the canal, which can be entered from Wandlebank by a wrought-iron gate to a bridge over the canal, which survives from Nelson's time. Wandle Park was then the grounds of Wandle Bank House, the home of Nelson's friend James Perry between 1790 and 1821. The park, which preserves a few traces of the house and monumental fountains, is now owned by the National Trust and managed by the London Borough of Merton. Perry, owner of Merton Mill and proprietor of the 'Morning Chronicle' newspaper, was one of the promoters of the Surrey Iron Railway, which ran north from here by way of Mead Path on the east side of the river to Wandsworth.

Wandsworth

From the north entrance to Wandle Park Mead Path can be reached via South Road (turn right from Park) and the left turn into Mead Road. The path runs well to the east of the Wandle, but partly by what seems to be a leat of the River Graveney, and provides wild flowers and water life. Most of the area between the path and the river is occupied by the South Wimbledon or Wandle Valley Sewage Works, established in 1877 on watermeadows known as Holmesmead and Bygrave Mead in 1512: small parties (with strong stomachs) can be taken round the works to observe the discharge into the river. There is also an access point to the Wandle on the opposite bank from the recreation ground in Garfield Road (reached from Haydons Road by a series of side streets bearing the names of poets).

Both Mead Path and Haydons Road lead to Plough Lane, where the Wandle can be viewed in both directions from the bridge. There is an ancient mill site to the north-east of the bridge (along Copper Mill Lane), which may mark the corn mill belonging to Merton Priory at Summerstown in 1150. It was the famous Garratt Copper Mills established by Dutch immigrants for at least the century after 1750, but had closed by 1895, although the wheel continued to be used by the successor leather works into the 1950s, and one very distinctive building remains.

Access to the next stretch of the river is mostly blocked by Wimbledon Stadium and extensive new development on the east bank, but it may be possible to obtain permission to reach the river from one of the firms along this side, and from the park-keeper in Garratt Park (off Garratt Lane at Siward Road) to cross the allotments between the park and the water. On the other side there may be access with permission through the grounds of the Wimbledon Sewage Works. In this area the Wandle is joined by its main tributary, the River Graveney, which rises in South Norwood and is supplemented by underground sources on its way across Wandsworth, but only appears above ground as it approaches the Wandle.

There were textile printing works here in the middle of the nineteenth century, but the next main mill sites (both approachable by turning left off Garratt Lane) are opposite the end of Trewint Street—the Garratt oil mills of the eighteenth and nineteenth centuries, perhaps on the location of a fifteenth-century fulling mill—and between Penwith and Duntshill Roads, where the river can be observed from two road bridges as it curves in its concrete bed into and under what is now the Kenco Coffee factory. During the nineteenth century there were silk and cloth printing works at Earlsfield, but these were converted to making street lamps in the 1920s.

From this point one should make one's way to the southern section of King George's Park, which has the Wandle flowing along its eastern side. This can be reached from Garratt Lane by way of the bridges at the far side of the Henry Prince Estate or Lydden Road; or from the west by continuing along Penwith or Strathville Roads to turn right onto Merton Road and then right again into Burr Road. From the Kimber Road exit from this part of the Park one can either follow the river to the east by way of Twilley Street to Garratt Lane; or, by turning left then right, enter a footpath leading between houses and a sports ground to the end of Brathway Road, from where the path continues across the side of the northern section of King George's Park. It is then possible to reach Garratt Lane either by continuing along the path to the bridge by the mill (now Benham and Son Ltd.) or by crossing to the swimming pool and the bridge at Mapleton Road.

In the centre of Wandsworth only occasional glimpses can be obtained of the river and the series of great mills which once stood along its banks. The course of the river has been constantly altered, first for the benefit of the mills, and more recently for modern redevelopment. At Buckhold Road (reached by turning right at the west end of Mapleton Road), as it approaches Wandsworth High Street, there was once a wooden bridge to take the Surrey Iron Railway before it looped back again across the river further upstream by a second wooden bridge. From this point it would seem that the river originally ran north past Wandsworth Church to the Frogmore inlet, but that a second stream, which the river now uses, ran parallel to the east, and connected with the basin, entered from the Thames by a lock and capable of holding thirty barges, where the Surrey Iron Railway terminated at Ram Field. The only real access points in this section are the bridges in Wandsworth High Street, allegedly first built at the command of Queen Elizabeth because she got her feet wet when crossing the Wandle on her way to her palace at Sheen, and in Armoury

The Wandle joins the Thames at Wandsworth. The mouth of the river, which once brought barges to the terminus of the Surrey Iron Railway, is not generally accessible to the public, but can be seen at a distance from The Causeway, leading off Armoury Way.

Photo by J. Jackson

Way, although permission may be gained to view the river from the famous Ram Brewery between these points. The Brewery contains two simple beam engines, one of 16 h.p. (1835), the other of 20 h.p. (1867), to drive the mashing and milling machinery.

A good deal of work remains to be done on the history of the Wandsworth mills, but four major sites can be identified, in addition to Gardiner's calico printing mill which in 1750 employed almost three-quarters of the working population. The uppermost mill along Garratt Lane by King George's Park was a paper mill during the nineteenth century, but had been reduced to varnish and gas-mantle factories by the present century. Nearer Wandsworth High Street was the first of the three great flour mills owned by Messrs. Watney and Wells during the nineteenth century, which between them worked 31 pairs of grindstones and produced some 60,000 sacks of flour a year. The importance of the Wandsworth flour mills for feeding London was recognised in 1610, when it was largely the opposition of the Wandsworth 'mealemen' which prevented a proportion of the river water being drawn off to supply the City. This Upper Mill may not, however, have existed at that period, since the earliest date recorded so far is 1740: it was later owned by George Pimm and was working until 1929. The building was finally demolished in 1962.

North of Wandsworth Bridge there was the Middle Mill by the railway basin; and close to the mouth of the river into the Thames stood the Lower (or Causeway) Mill, which was partly a tide mill. All this very desolate but interesting area can now be seen from The Causeway (off Armoury Way), and from the point where there is still a spectacular fall of water under the modern Central Electricity Generating Board building it is possible to look out over the last few yards of the Wandle as it enters the Thames. For a closer inspection of what is also a most important area archaeologically it would be necessary to enter the refuse depot at Frogmore on one side, and the Gas Board land on the other.

SELECT GUIDE TO FURTHER READING

(Items under each heading are arranged in chronological order of publication)

General Historical Works

W. Camden - - - - *Britannia* ([1586] ed. R. Gough: London, 1806).

D. Defoe - - - - *A Tour Through the Whole Island of Great Britain* (London, 1724-26; Everyman edition, 1962).

J. Aubrey - - - - *Natural History and Antiquities of the County of Surrey* (London, 1718-19).

J. Edwards - - - - *Companion from London to Brighthelmston* (Dorking, 1789; 2nd ed., 1804).

D. Lysons - - - - *The Environs of London* (London, 1792; 2nd ed., 1811).

J. Malcolm - - - - *Compendium of Modern Husbandry* (London, 1805).

J. Hassell - - - - *Picturesque Rides and Walks* (London, 1817-18).

S. Lewis - - - - - *A Topographical Dictionary of England* (London, 1831).

E. W. Brayley - - - - *A Topographical History of Surrey* (London, 1841-48).

Victoria County History of Surrey (London, 1903-12).

N. Pevsner & I. Nairn - - *The Buildings of England: Surrey* (Penguin, 1962).

The Wandle

Books

C. R. B. Barrett - - - *Surrey: Highways, Byways and Waterways* (London, 1895).

J. M. Hobson - - - - *The Book of the Wandle* (London, 1924).

R. T. Hopkins - - - - *Old Watermills and Windmills* (London, [1938]).

J. Hillier - - - - *Old Surrey Watermills* (London, 1951).

N. J. Barton - - - - *The Lost Rivers of London* (London, 1962).

Articles

F. Braithwaite - - - - 'On the Rise and Fall of the River Wandle,' *Proceedings of the Institution of Civil Engineers*, xx (1860-61), 191-258.

Dewey-Bates - - - - 'On the Wandle,' *English Illustrated Magazine* (1889), 636-44.

M. S. Giuseppi - - - 'The River Wandle in 1610,' *Surrey Archaeological Collections*, xxi (1908), 170-191; 'The River Wandle: Past and Present,' *Wimbledon and Merton Annual* (1910), 9-47.

W. Whitaker - - - - 'The Water Supply of Surrey,' *Memoirs of the Geological Survey* (1912).

Report of River Wandle Open Spaces Committee (1914).

Report of Inspector, Board of Agriculture and Fisheries (1918-19).

R.H.B. - - - - - 'Where London still has Water Power: The Wandle, a River of Mills' [newspaper cutting, n.d.: Wallington Library].

J. E. Nash - - - - *Effect of Flood Elimination Works on the River Wandle* (1958).

A. E. Bensusan - - - 'No Clearer or Diviner Water,' *The Lady* (1962), 682-690.

M. J. Wilks - - - - *A Check-List of Wandle Watermills* (Carshalton, 1967).

D. Harvey - - - - 'Lesser Known Surrey Rivers: I. The Wandle,' *Surrey*, ii, 3 (1971), 32-33.

G.L.C. - - - - - *Annual Report of the Scientific Adviser* (G.L.C., Published annually).

Geology

J. W. Bazalgette - - - *The Wandle Valley Drainage* (1873).

G. J. Hinde - - - - 'Notes on the Gravels of Croydon and its Neighbourhood,' *Proceedings of the Croydon Natural History and Scientific Society,* iv (1897), 219-233.

A. J. Jukes-Brown - - - 'The Cretaceous Rocks of Britain: III. The Upper Chalk of England,' *Memoirs of the Geological Survey* (1904).

A. J. Hogg - - - - 'Mitcham Gravels and their Mammalian Remains,' *Proceedings of the CNH & SS,* vi (1906), 133-141.

H. Dewey & C. E. N. Bromehead 'The Geology of South London,' *Memoirs of the Geological Survey* (1921).

C. C. Fagg - - - - *Regional Survey Atlas of Croydon and District* (Croydon, 1936-); 'The Recession of the Chalk Escarpment and the Development of Chalk Valleys in the Regional Survey Area,' *Proceedings of the CNH & SS,* x (1923), 93-112 = xv (1972), 1-20; 'The Coombes and Embayments of the Chalk Escarpment,' *ibid.,* xii (1954), 117-131.

S. W. Wooldridge & D. Linton - *Structure, Surface and Drainage in South East England* (London, 1955).

D. S. Peake - - - - 'The Age of the Wandle Gravels in the Vicinity of Croydon,' *Proceedings of the CNH & SS,* xiv (1971), 145-161.

P. J. Osborne - - - - 'The Insect Faunas of the Organic Deposits within the Wandle Gravels,' *ibid.,* 162-175.

P. W. Sowan - - - - 'Elephas Primigenius found at West Croydon,' *ibid.,* 188-190.

J. Docherty - - - - 'Chalk Karst,' *ibid.,* xv (1972), 21-34.

Croydon

J. C. Anderson - - - *Croydon, Prehistoric and Roman* (Croydon, 1874); *A Short Chronicle concerning the Parish of Croydon* (Croydon, 1882).

B. Latham - - - - 'Croydon Bourne Flows,' *Proceedings of the CNH & SS,* vi (1904); 'A Chapter in the History of Croydon,' *ibid.,* vi (1909), 137-240; 'Records of Underground Water and Croydon Bourne Flows,' *ibid.,* viii (1917), 113-125.

I. D. Margary - - - - *Roman Ways in the Weald* (London, 1948).

D. W. Blackmore - - - 'The Rebirth of Croydon in 1851,' *Proceedings of the CNH & SS,* xii (1954), 95-116.

J. Batley - - - - 'The Bourne through the Ages,' *Bourne Society Local History Records,* i (1962); 'The Legend of the Woe Water,' *Croydon Advertiser* (6 December, 1968).

J. B. Gent (ed.) - - - *Croydon: The Story of a Hundred Years* (Croydon, 1970).

R. C. W. Cox - - - - 'The Old Centre of Croydon: Victorian Decay and Redevelopment,' *Perspectives in English Urban History* (ed. A. Everitt: London, 1973).

B. J. Salter (ed.) - - - *Central Croydon* (Croydon, 1973).

K. M. Newbury - - - 'The Bourne Through the Ages,' *Bourne Society Local History Records,* xiii (1974).

Sutton

J. Williams - - - - *Historical Notes on Wallington* (London and Wallington, 1873).

G. B. Brightling - - - *Some Particulars Relating to the History and Antiquities of Carshalton* (Bethnal Green, 1872; 2nd ed., 1882).

A. Smee - - - - - *My Garden: Its Plan and Culture* (London, 1872).

T. Bentham - - - - *A History of Beddington* (London, 1923).

C. P. Lovelock - - - 'Carshalton's River,' *Ruskin Monthly*, iii, 21-22 (1923).

A. E. Jones - - - - *From Medieval Manor to London Suburb: An Obituary of Carshalton* (Carshalton, 1970); *An Illustrated Directory of Old Carshalton* (Carshalton, 1973).

Archaeological and historical bibliographies will be found in the following brochures: Beddington, Carshalton and Wallington Archaeological Society Jubilee, 1970; *Caring for Carshalton* (Carshalton Society, 1973).

Merton

E. M. Jowett - - - - *History of Merton and Morden* (Merton and Morden, 1951).

W. H. Prentis - - - - *The Snuff-Mill Story* (Mitcham, 1970).

R. J. Milward - - - - *History of Wimbledon* (Wimbledon, 1970-).

E. N. Montague - - - *History of Mitcham Common* (Mitcham, 1970); 'Mitcham Bridge, the Watermeads and the Wandle,' *Mitcham News* (16 and 30 July, 1971).

E. M. Jowett - - - - 'The Wandle,' *Merton & Morden/Mitcham/Wimbledon News* (17 and 24 August, 1973).

Wandsworth

C. T. Davis - - - - *The Industries of Wandsworth, Past and Present* (1898).

Anon. - - - - - 'The Mealemen of Wandsworth together with some account of the River Wandle,' *Wandsworth Borough News Handbook* (1911).

Various articles can also be found in *Wandsworth Notes,* vols. i, iv and xii; and *Wandsworth Borough News* for 1970 and 1971; and the *Wandsworth Historian:* a list is available from Wandsworth Reference Library.

Surrey Iron Railway

J. Priestley - - - - *Historical Account of Navigable Rivers, Canals and Railways throughout Great Britain* ([1830] Newton Abbot, 1969).

C. E. Lee - - - - 'Early Railways in Surrey,' *Transactions of the Newcomen Society*, xxi (1940-41).

C. F. Dendy Marshall - - *History of the Southern Railway* (London, 1937; 2nd ed., 1963).

H. P. White - - - - *Regional History of the Railways of Great Britain: III. Greater London* (London, 1963).

B. Baxter - - - - *Stone Blocks and Iron Rails* (Newton Abbot, 1966), which contains a further bibliography.

Source material for the foregoing and further information may be obtained from the following.

London Borough of
CROYDON

Reference Library, Katharine Street, Croydon, CR9 1ET (01-688 3627).

London Borough of
LAMBETH

Minet Library, 52 Knatchbull Road, SE5 9QY (01-274 5325).

London Borough of
MERTON

Mitcham Library, London Road, Mitcham, CR4 2YR (01-648 4070/6516).
Morden Library, Morden Road, SW19 3DA (01-542 2842/1701).
Wimbledon Library, Wimbledon Hill Road, SW19 7NB (01-946 7979/7432).

SURREY COUNTY COUNCIL

Surrey Records Office, County Hall, Penrhyn Road, Kingston upon Thames, K21 2DN (01-546 1050 Ext. 179).

London Borough of
SUTTON

Carshalton Library, The Square, Carshalton, SM5 3BN (01-647 1151/2).
Wallington Library, Shotfield, Wallington, SM6 0HY (01-647 4458/9).

London Borough of
WANDSWORTH

West Hill Library, West Hill, SW18 1RZ (01-874 1143/5).

THE WANDLE GROUP

The Wandle Group was formed on the 13th September, 1973, and holds regular meetings in Wallington Public Library. It consists of representatives of local amenity, historical, natural history and other interested societies, as well as libraries and record offices holding Wandle material. It aims to co-ordinate the activities and research of these organisations, to encourage such research, to protect and improve the Wandle, to promote the publication of material relating to it, and by these means to stimulate public interest in all aspects of the river and its history.

Chairman: D. J. S. Cluett, Wallington Library, Shotfield, Wallington (01-647 4458)

Secretary: R. C. Twilley, 'Felstead,' Green Lane, Chessington, Surrey, KT9 2DT (01-397 4926; School 01-946 5452)

MEMBER SOCIETIES AND ORGANISATIONS

(W.R. = Wandle Representative)

THE BOURNE SOCIETY

Hon. Sec.: Miss D. Tutt, 16 Warren Park, Warlingham, Surrey, CR3 9LB.

W.R.: Mr. J. C. Batley, 7A Burntwood Lane, Caterham, Surrey (22 43527).

BEDDINGTON, CARSHALTON AND WALLINGTON ARCHAEOLOGICAL SOCIETY

Hon. Sec.: Miss D. M. Andrews, 7 Bute Gardens West, Wallington, Surrey (01-647 8161).

W.R.: Mr. R. A. Michell, 24 Carleton Avenue, Wallington, Surrey (01-647 4896).

THE CARSHALTON SOCIETY

Hon. Sec.: Mr. J. S. Thornton, 25 Lavender Road, Carshalton, Surrey (01-647 2574).

W.R.: Professor M. J. Wilks, 9 Talbot Road, Carshalton, Surrey (01-647 1356).

CROYDON FRIENDS OF THE EARTH

Hon. Sec.: Mr. C. Conroy, 58A Coomb Road, Croydon, Surrey.

W.R.: Mr. C. J. Monk, c/o 52 Ashburton Avenue, Croydon, Surrey, CR0 7JE.

CROYDON NATURAL HISTORY AND SCIENTIFIC SOCIETY

Hon. Sec.: Mr. P. Sowan, 96A Brighton Road, South Croydon, Surrey, CR2 6AD (01-681 6194).

W.R.: As above.

THE JOHN EVELYN SOCIETY

Hon. Sec.: Mr. E. F. Peeler, 109 Pepys Road, S.W.20 (01-946 7017).

W.R.: Mr. J. H. North, 6 Clare Court, Grosvenor Hill, S.W.19 (01-946 0699).

GREATER LONDON INDUSTRIAL ARCHAEOLOGY SOCIETY

Hon. Sec.: Miss V. Glass, 69 St. Peters Road, Croydon, Surrey, CR0 1HS (01-686 4003).

W.R.: Mr. I. Bradley, A.L.A., Flat 3, 12 Cedar Road, Sutton, Surrey, SM2 5DA.

GROSVENOR YOUNG NATURALISTS SOCIETY

Hon. Sec.: c/o 6 Osmond Gardens, Wallington, Surrey, SM6 8SM (01-647 6466).

W.R.: As above.

MERTON HISTORICAL SOCIETY

Hon. Sec.: Miss E. F. Waugh, 24 Mostyn Road, London, S.W.19.

W.R.: Mr. Harris, 239 Tamworth Lane, Mitcham, Surrey.

MERTON PUBLIC LIBRARIES

Borough Librarian: Mr. E. J. Adsett, F.L.A.

W.R.: Mr. C. A. Toase, A.L.A., Senior Reference Librarian, Wimbledon Reference Library, Wimbledon Hill Road, SW19 7NB (01-946 7979/7432).

THE PURE RIVERS SOCIETY

Hon. Sec.: Mr. J. R. Fleetwood, 74 Dagenham Avenue, Dagenham, Essex, RM9 6LH.

W.R.: Mr. A. Brown, 89 Ravensbury Road, London, S.W.18 (01-946 4024).

SPENCER PARK TEACHERS' CENTRE
(Wandsworth, S.W.18)

Hon. Sec.: Mr. A. R. Knight, 34 Lawrence Park, Ham, Richmond, Surrey (01-940 8695).

W.R.: As above. (Teachers' Centre 01-870 2486).

SURREY ARCHAEOLOGICAL SOCIETY

Hon. Sec.: Mr. D. J. Turner, 21 Evesham Road, Reigate, Surrey, RH2 9DC (Reigate 48158).

W.R.: Mr. E. N. Montague, 9 Devonshire Road, Sutton, Surrey.

SURREY RECORD OFFICE

County Archivist: Miss M. Gollancz, M.A., County Hall, Kingston upon Thames, KT1 2DN (01-546 1050).

W.R.: As above.

SUTTON FRIENDS OF THE EARTH

Hon. Sec.: Mrs. J. Coker, 5 Fairford Court, Grange Road, Sutton, Surrey.

W.R.: As above.

SUTTON PUBLIC LIBRARIES

Borough Librarian: Mr. Roy P. Smith, F.L.A.

W.R.: Mr. D. J. S. Cluett, A.L.A., Senior Reference Librarian, Wallington Reference Library, Shotfield, Wallington, Surrey, SM6 0HY (01-647 4458).

WANDSWORTH ANGLING SOCIETY

Hon. Sec.: Mr. A. C. M. Brown, 89 Ravensbury Road, S.W.18.

W.R.: Mr. R. A. Lockyer, 477 Gander Green Lane, North Cheam, SM3 9RA (01-644 2892).

WANDSWORTH HISTORICAL SOCIETY

Hon. Sec.: Mr. D. R. Pollock, 102 Disraeli Road, Putney, S.W.15 (01-788 5687).

W.R.: Mr. G. Munro, 145 Melrose Avenue, London, SW19 8AU.

WANDSWORTH PUBLIC LIBRARIES

Borough Librarian: Mr. E. V. Cobett, M.A., F.L.A., F.R.S.A.

W.R.: Mr. R. A. Shaw, A.L.A., Local History Librarian, West Hill Public Library, West Hill, SW18 1RZ (01-874 1143).

WATERMEADS TRUST (NATIONAL TRUST)

Hon. Sec.: Mrs. W. M. Sibthorpe, 54A Wandle Road, Morden, Surrey (01-648 6403).

W.R.: As above.